To Imani,
May all your going
& doing align with all your
goals & dreams!
Carolyn 202

These specific ISBN numbers have been filed with the library of congress for copywriting purposes of this publication.

979-8-9858540-0-8 paperback
979-8-9858540-1-5 paperback journal
979-8-9858540-2-2 kindle
979-8-9858540-3-9 epub

Cover design and layout design by: A. Payne's Designs
Amber Mabry | amber@apaynedesigns.com

DIAMONDS & PEARLS: AFFIRMATIONS OF A MOMPRENEUR WHO ROCKS!
D&P

Mompreneur
Organizer

This journal is an invitation for you to dream, explore, get organized and thrive as a woman, mother and mompreneur.

Mompreneurs are ever growing and changing. If you run out of space treat yourself (and a friend) to a new journal!

Career Plan

PLAN PERIOD: DATE:

CURRENT POSITION

GOALS

SHORT TERM GOALS

MID TERM GOALS

LONG TERM GOALS

HOW I'LL MAKE IT HAPPEN

CURRENT SKILLS EXPERIENCE KNOWLEDGE

NEW SKILLS EXPERIENCE KNOWLEDGE REQUIRED

Career Plan

PLAN PERIOD: DATE:

CURRENT POSITION

GOALS

SHORT TERM GOALS

MID TERM GOALS

LONG TERM GOALS

HOW I'LL MAKE IT HAPPEN

CURRENT SKILLS EXPERIENCE KNOWLEDGE

NEW SKILLS EXPERIENCE KNOWLEDGE REQUIRED

Prayer Journal

Today's Passage

Key Verses / Key Points

Preacher:
Sermon Topic:

Prayer

Notes

Prayer Journal

Today's Passage

Key Verses / Key Points

Preacher:
Sermon Topic:

Prayer

Notes

MONTHLY *To Do* LIST

January

February

March

April

May

June

MONTHLY To Do LIST

July

August

September

October

November

December

MONTHLY To Do LIST

January

February

March

April

May

June

MONTHLY *To Do* LIST

July	August
☐	☐
☐	☐
☐	☐
☐	☐
☐	☐

September	October
☐	☐
☐	☐
☐	☐
☐	☐
☐	☐

November	December
☐	☐
☐	☐
☐	☐
☐	☐
☐	☐

Savings Tracker

Saving For:

DATE	DEPOSIT	AMOUNT

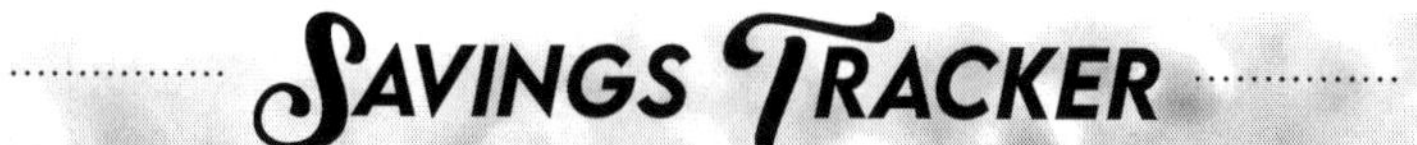

Saving For:

DATE	DEPOSIT	AMOUNT

Savings Tracker

Saving For:

DATE	DEPOSIT	AMOUNT

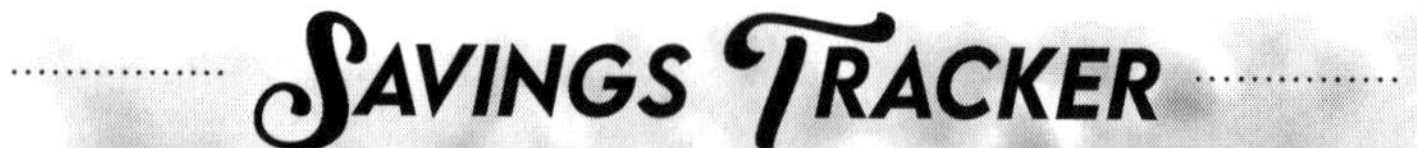

Saving For:

DATE	DEPOSIT	AMOUNT

Bill Tracker

BILL AMOUNT	DUE DATE	DATE PAID

Bill Tracker

BILL AMOUNT	DUE DATE	DATE PAID

Bill Tracker

BILL AMOUNT	DUE DATE	DATE PAID

Bill Tracker

BILL AMOUNT	DUE DATE	DATE PAID

Personal Expense Tracker

MONTH: YEAR:

DATE	EXPENSE DESCRIPTION	PAYMENT TYPE	AMOUNT

Personal Expense Tracker

MONTH: YEAR:

DATE	EXPENSE DESCRIPTION	PAYMENT TYPE	AMOUNT

Personal Expense Tracker

MONTH: YEAR:

DATE	EXPENSE DESCRIPTION	PAYMENT TYPE	AMOUNT

Personal Expense Tracker

MONTH:		YEAR:	
DATE	EXPENSE DESCRIPTION	PAYMENT TYPE	AMOUNT

Utilities Tracker

COMPANY NAME: ______________________________

ACCOUNT #: ______________________________

DUE DATE: ______________________________

CUSTOMER SERVICE #: ______________________________

EMERGENCY #: ______________________________

BILLING ADDRESS: ______________________________

URL: ______________________________

USERNAME: ______________________________

PASSWORD: ______________________________

NOTES ______________________________

____

COMPANY NAME: ______________________________

ACCOUNT #: ______________________________

DUE DATE: ______________________________

CUSTOMER SERVICE #: ______________________________

EMERGENCY #: ______________________________

BILLING ADDRESS: ______________________________

URL: ______________________________

USERNAME: ______________________________

PASSWORD: ______________________________

NOTES ______________________________

____

Utilities Tracker

COMPANY NAME: ______________________________

ACCOUNT #: ______________________________

DUE DATE: ______________________________

CUSTOMER SERVICE #: ______________________________

EMERGENCY #: ______________________________

BILLING ADDRESS: ______________________________

URL: ______________________________

USERNAME: ______________________________

PASSWORD: ______________________________

NOTES ______________________________

____

COMPANY NAME: ______________________________

ACCOUNT #: ______________________________

DUE DATE: ______________________________

CUSTOMER SERVICE #: ______________________________

EMERGENCY #: ______________________________

BILLING ADDRESS: ______________________________

URL: ______________________________

USERNAME: ______________________________

PASSWORD: ______________________________

NOTES ______________________________

____

Utilities Tracker

COMPANY NAME: ______________________________

ACCOUNT #: ______________________________

DUE DATE: ______________________________

CUSTOMER SERVICE #: ______________________________

EMERGENCY #: ______________________________

BILLING ADDRESS: ______________________________

URL: ______________________________

USERNAME: ______________________________

PASSWORD: ______________________________

NOTES ______________________________

____

COMPANY NAME: ______________________________

ACCOUNT #: ______________________________

DUE DATE: ______________________________

CUSTOMER SERVICE #: ______________________________

EMERGENCY #: ______________________________

BILLING ADDRESS: ______________________________

URL: ______________________________

USERNAME: ______________________________

PASSWORD: ______________________________

NOTES ______________________________

____

Utilities Tracker

COMPANY NAME: ______________________________

ACCOUNT #: ______________________________

DUE DATE: ______________________________

CUSTOMER SERVICE #: ______________________________

EMERGENCY #: ______________________________

BILLING ADDRESS: ______________________________

URL: ______________________________

USERNAME: ______________________________

PASSWORD: ______________________________

NOTES ______________________________

____

COMPANY NAME: ______________________________

ACCOUNT #: ______________________________

DUE DATE: ______________________________

CUSTOMER SERVICE #: ______________________________

EMERGENCY #: ______________________________

BILLING ADDRESS: ______________________________

URL: ______________________________

USERNAME: ______________________________

PASSWORD: ______________________________

NOTES ______________________________

____

Utilities Tracker

BILL AMOUNT	DUE DATE	DATE PAID

Utilities Tracker

BILL AMOUNT	DUE DATE	DATE PAID

Utilities Tracker

BILL AMOUNT	DUE DATE	DATE PAID

Utilities Tracker

BILL AMOUNT	DUE DATE	DATE PAID

Password Tracker

WEBSITE	USERNAME	PASSWORD

Password Tracker

WEBSITE	USERNAME	PASSWORD

Password Tracker

WEBSITE	USERNAME	PASSWORD

Password Tracker

WEBSITE	USERNAME	PASSWORD

Chores List

CHORE	FREQUENCY	PERSON IN CHARGE

CHORES LIST

CHORE	FREQUENCY	PERSON IN CHARGE

CHORES LIST

CHORE	FREQUENCY	PERSON IN CHARGE

Chores List

CHORE	FREQUENCY	PERSON IN CHARGE

CLEANING *Check* LIST

January	February
☐	☐
☐	☐
☐	☐
☐	☐
☐	☐

March	April
☐	☐
☐	☐
☐	☐
☐	☐
☐	☐

May	June
☐	☐
☐	☐
☐	☐
☐	☐
☐	☐

CLEANING *Check* LIST

July	August
☐	☐
☐	☐
☐	☐
☐	☐
☐	☐

September	October
☐	☐
☐	☐
☐	☐
☐	☐
☐	☐

November	December
☐	☐
☐	☐
☐	☐
☐	☐
☐	☐

CLEANING *Check* LIST

January	February
☐	☐
☐	☐
☐	☐
☐	☐
☐	☐

March	April
☐	☐
☐	☐
☐	☐
☐	☐
☐	☐

May	June
☐	☐
☐	☐
☐	☐
☐	☐
☐	☐

CLEANING *Check* LIST

July	August
☐	☐
☐	☐
☐	☐
☐	☐
☐	☐

September	October
☐	☐
☐	☐
☐	☐
☐	☐
☐	☐

November	December
☐	☐
☐	☐
☐	☐
☐	☐
☐	☐

Meal Prep

	BREAKFAST	LUNCH	DINNER
MONDAY			
TUESDAY			
WEDNESDAY			
THURSDAY			
FRIDAY			
SATURDAY			
SUNDAY			

	BREAKFAST	LUNCH	DINNER
MONDAY			
TUESDAY			
WEDNESDAY			
THURSDAY			
FRIDAY			
SATURDAY			
SUNDAY			

Meal Prep

	BREAKFAST	LUNCH	DINNER
MONDAY			
TUESDAY			
WEDNESDAY			
THURSDAY			
FRIDAY			
SATURDAY			
SUNDAY			

	BREAKFAST	LUNCH	DINNER
MONDAY			
TUESDAY			
WEDNESDAY			
THURSDAY			
FRIDAY			
SATURDAY			
SUNDAY			

Food Journal

Breakfast	Servings	Calories	
		Subtotal	
Snack			
		Subtotal	
Lunch			
		Subtotal	
Snack			
		Subtotal	
Dinner			
		Subtotal	
Snack			
		Subtotal	

Total Calories From Food

FITNESS ACTIVITY JOURNAL

	Duration	Calories

Total Calories From Fitness

NOTES

Food Journal

Breakfast

	Servings	Calories	
		Subtotal	

Snack

		Subtotal	

Lunch

		Subtotal	

Snack

		Subtotal	

Dinner

		Subtotal	

Snack

		Subtotal	

Total Calories From Food

FITNESS ACTIVITY JOURNAL

	Duration	Calories

Total Calories From Fitness

NOTES

Food Journal

Breakfast	Servings	Calories	
		Subtotal	

Snack			
		Subtotal	

Lunch			
		Subtotal	

Snack			
		Subtotal	

Dinner			
		Subtotal	

Snack			
		Subtotal	

Total Calories From Food

FITNESS ACTIVITY JOURNAL

	Duration	Calories

Total Calories From Fitness

NOTES

Food Journal

Breakfast

	Servings	Calories	
		Subtotal	

Snack

	Servings	Calories	
		Subtotal	

Lunch

	Servings	Calories	
		Subtotal	

Snack

	Servings	Calories	
		Subtotal	

Dinner

	Servings	Calories	
		Subtotal	

Snack

	Servings	Calories	
		Subtotal	

Total Calories From Food ____________

FITNESS ACTIVITY JOURNAL

	Duration	Calories

Total Calories From Fitness ____________

NOTES

Fitness Calendar

Fill the days to keep track of your fitness goals.

January

S	M	T	W	T	F	S
						1
2	3	4	5	6	7	8
9	10	11	12	13	14	15
16	17	18	19	20	21	22
23	24	25	26	27	28	29
30	31					

February

S	M	T	W	T	F	S
		1	2	3	4	5
6	7	8	9	10	11	12
13	14	15	16	17	18	19
20	21	22	23	24	25	26
27	28					

March

S	M	T	W	T	F	S
		1	2	3	4	5
6	7	8	9	10	11	12
13	14	15	16	17	18	19
20	21	22	23	24	25	26
27	28	29	30	31		

April

S	M	T	W	T	F	S
					1	2
3	4	5	6	7	8	9
10	11	12	13	14	15	16
17	18	19	20	21	22	23
24	25	26	27	28	29	30

May

S	M	T	W	T	F	S
1	2	3	4	5	6	7
8	9	10	11	12	13	14
15	16	17	18	19	20	21
22	23	24	25	26	27	28
29	30	31				

June

S	M	T	W	T	F	S
			1	2	3	4
5	6	7	8	9	10	11
12	13	14	15	16	17	18
19	20	21	22	23	24	25
26	27	28	29	30		

July

S	M	T	W	T	F	S
					1	2
3	4	5	6	7	8	9
10	11	12	13	14	15	16
17	18	19	20	21	22	23
24	25	26	27	28	29	30
31						

August

S	M	T	W	T	F	S
	1	2	3	4	5	6
7	8	9	10	11	12	13
14	15	16	17	18	19	20
21	22	23	24	25	26	27
28	29	30	31			

September

S	M	T	W	T	F	S
				1	2	3
4	5	6	7	8	9	10
11	12	13	14	15	16	17
18	19	20	21	22	23	24
25	26	27	28	29	30	

October

S	M	T	W	T	F	S
						1
2	3	4	5	6	7	8
9	10	11	12	13	14	15
16	17	18	19	20	21	22
23	24	25	26	27	28	29
30	31					

November

S	M	T	W	T	F	S
		1	2	3	4	5
6	7	8	9	10	11	12
13	14	15	16	17	18	19
20	21	22	23	24	25	26
27	28	29	30			

December

S	M	T	W	T	F	S
				1	2	3
4	5	6	7	8	9	10
11	12	13	14	15	16	17
18	19	20	21	22	23	24
25	26	27	28	29	30	31

Fitness Calendar

Fill the days to keep track of your fitness goals.

January

S	M	T	W	T	F	S
						1
2	3	4	5	6	7	8
9	10	11	12	13	14	15
16	17	18	19	20	21	22
23	24	25	26	27	28	29
30	31					

February

S	M	T	W	T	F	S
		1	2	3	4	5
6	7	8	9	10	11	12
13	14	15	16	17	18	19
20	21	22	23	24	25	26
27	28					

March

S	M	T	W	T	F	S
		1	2	3	4	5
6	7	8	9	10	11	12
13	14	15	16	17	18	19
20	21	22	23	24	25	26
27	28	29	30	31		

April

S	M	T	W	T	F	S
					1	2
3	4	5	6	7	8	9
10	11	12	13	14	15	16
17	18	19	20	21	22	23
24	25	26	27	28	29	30

May

S	M	T	W	T	F	S
1	2	3	4	5	6	7
8	9	10	11	12	13	14
15	16	17	18	19	20	21
22	23	24	25	26	27	28
29	30	31				

June

S	M	T	W	T	F	S
			1	2	3	4
5	6	7	8	9	10	11
12	13	14	15	16	17	18
19	20	21	22	23	24	25
26	27	28	29	30		

July

S	M	T	W	T	F	S
					1	2
3	4	5	6	7	8	9
10	11	12	13	14	15	16
17	18	19	20	21	22	23
24	25	26	27	28	29	30
31						

August

S	M	T	W	T	F	S
	1	2	3	4	5	6
7	8	9	10	11	12	13
14	15	16	17	18	19	20
21	22	23	24	25	26	27
28	29	30	31			

September

S	M	T	W	T	F	S
				1	2	3
4	5	6	7	8	9	10
11	12	13	14	15	16	17
18	19	20	21	22	23	24
25	26	27	28	29	30	

October

S	M	T	W	T	F	S
						1
2	3	4	5	6	7	8
9	10	11	12	13	14	15
16	17	18	19	20	21	22
23	24	25	26	27	28	29
30	31					

November

S	M	T	W	T	F	S
		1	2	3	4	5
6	7	8	9	10	11	12
13	14	15	16	17	18	19
20	21	22	23	24	25	26
27	28	29	30			

December

S	M	T	W	T	F	S
				1	2	3
4	5	6	7	8	9	10
11	12	13	14	15	16	17
18	19	20	21	22	23	24
25	26	27	28	29	30	31

Fitness Calendar

Fill the days to keep track of your fitness goals.

January

S	M	T	W	T	F	S
						1
2	3	4	5	6	7	8
9	10	11	12	13	14	15
16	17	18	19	20	21	22
23	24	25	26	27	28	29
30	31					

February

S	M	T	W	T	F	S
		1	2	3	4	5
6	7	8	9	10	11	12
13	14	15	16	17	18	19
20	21	22	23	24	25	26
27	28					

March

S	M	T	W	T	F	S
		1	2	3	4	5
6	7	8	9	10	11	12
13	14	15	16	17	18	19
20	21	22	23	24	25	26
27	28	29	30	31		

April

S	M	T	W	T	F	S
					1	2
3	4	5	6	7	8	9
10	11	12	13	14	15	16
17	18	19	20	21	22	23
24	25	26	27	28	29	30

May

S	M	T	W	T	F	S
1	2	3	4	5	6	7
8	9	10	11	12	13	14
15	16	17	18	19	20	21
22	23	24	25	26	27	28
29	30	31				

June

S	M	T	W	T	F	S
			1	2	3	4
5	6	7	8	9	10	11
12	13	14	15	16	17	18
19	20	21	22	23	24	25
26	27	28	29	30		

July

S	M	T	W	T	F	S
					1	2
3	4	5	6	7	8	9
10	11	12	13	14	15	16
17	18	19	20	21	22	23
24	25	26	27	28	29	30
31						

August

S	M	T	W	T	F	S
	1	2	3	4	5	6
7	8	9	10	11	12	13
14	15	16	17	18	19	20
21	22	23	24	25	26	27
28	29	30	31			

September

S	M	T	W	T	F	S
				1	2	3
4	5	6	7	8	9	10
11	12	13	14	15	16	17
18	19	20	21	22	23	24
25	26	27	28	29	30	

October

S	M	T	W	T	F	S
						1
2	3	4	5	6	7	8
9	10	11	12	13	14	15
16	17	18	19	20	21	22
23	24	25	26	27	28	29
30	31					

November

S	M	T	W	T	F	S
		1	2	3	4	5
6	7	8	9	10	11	12
13	14	15	16	17	18	19
20	21	22	23	24	25	26
27	28	29	30			

December

S	M	T	W	T	F	S
				1	2	3
4	5	6	7	8	9	10
11	12	13	14	15	16	17
18	19	20	21	22	23	24
25	26	27	28	29	30	31

Fitness Calendar

Fill the days to keep track of your fitness goals.

January

S	M	T	W	T	F	S
						1
2	3	4	5	6	7	8
9	10	11	12	13	14	15
16	17	18	19	20	21	22
23	24	25	26	27	28	29
30	31					

February

S	M	T	W	T	F	S
		1	2	3	4	5
6	7	8	9	10	11	12
13	14	15	16	17	18	19
20	21	22	23	24	25	26
27	28					

March

S	M	T	W	T	F	S
		1	2	3	4	5
6	7	8	9	10	11	12
13	14	15	16	17	18	19
20	21	22	23	24	25	26
27	28	29	30	31		

April

S	M	T	W	T	F	S
					1	2
3	4	5	6	7	8	9
10	11	12	13	14	15	16
17	18	19	20	21	22	23
24	25	26	27	28	29	30

May

S	M	T	W	T	F	S
1	2	3	4	5	6	7
8	9	10	11	12	13	14
15	16	17	18	19	20	21
22	23	24	25	26	27	28
29	30	31				

June

S	M	T	W	T	F	S
			1	2	3	4
5	6	7	8	9	10	11
12	13	14	15	16	17	18
19	20	21	22	23	24	25
26	27	28	29	30		

July

S	M	T	W	T	F	S
					1	2
3	4	5	6	7	8	9
10	11	12	13	14	15	16
17	18	19	20	21	22	23
24	25	26	27	28	29	30
31						

August

S	M	T	W	T	F	S
	1	2	3	4	5	6
7	8	9	10	11	12	13
14	15	16	17	18	19	20
21	22	23	24	25	26	27
28	29	30	31			

September

S	M	T	W	T	F	S
				1	2	3
4	5	6	7	8	9	10
11	12	13	14	15	16	17
18	19	20	21	22	23	24
25	26	27	28	29	30	

October

S	M	T	W	T	F	S
						1
2	3	4	5	6	7	8
9	10	11	12	13	14	15
16	17	18	19	20	21	22
23	24	25	26	27	28	29
30	31					

November

S	M	T	W	T	F	S
		1	2	3	4	5
6	7	8	9	10	11	12
13	14	15	16	17	18	19
20	21	22	23	24	25	26
27	28	29	30			

December

S	M	T	W	T	F	S
				1	2	3
4	5	6	7	8	9	10
11	12	13	14	15	16	17
18	19	20	21	22	23	24
25	26	27	28	29	30	31

Self Care

This Week Moto ______________________________

____

Self-Care Practices	Mon	Tue	Wen	Thu	Fri	Sat	Sun

Self Care

This Week Moto ______________________________

____

Self-Care Practices	Mon	Tue	Wen	Thu	Fri	Sat	Sun

Self Care

This Week Moto

Self-Care Practices	Mon	Tue	Wen	Thu	Fri	Sat	Sun

Self Care

This Week Moto ______________________________

____

Self-Care Practices	Mon	Tue	Wen	Thu	Fri	Sat	Sun

Babysitter Info

Emergency:

Parents:

Where we'll be:

Cell Phone:

Emergency

Phone #:

Child 1

Allergies

Child 2

Allergies

Child 3

Allergies

Child 4

Allergies

To Do:

- [ ]
- [ ]
- [ ]
- [ ]
- [ ]
- [ ]
- [ ]
- [ ]
- [ ]
- [ ]
- [ ]
- [ ]

Meals:

No No:

Snacks:

Rules:

Bedtime:

Notes:

Babysitter Info

Emergency: ____________________

Parents:

Where we'll be: ____________________

Cell Phone: ____________________

Emergency

Phone #: ____________________

Child 1 ____________________

Allergies ____________________

Child 2 ____________________

Allergies ____________________

Child 3

Allergies ____________________

Child 4 ____________________

Allergies ____________________

To Do:

- [ ] ____________________
- [ ] ____________________
- [ ] ____________________
- [ ] ____________________
- [ ] ____________________
- [ ] ____________________
- [ ] ____________________
- [ ] ____________________
- [ ] ____________________
- [ ] ____________________
- [ ] ____________________
- [ ] ____________________

Meals: ____________________

____

No No: ____________________

Snacks: ____________________

Rules: ____________________

____

Bedtime: ____________________

____

Notes: ____________________

____

____

Babysitter Info

To Do:

- [ ]
- [ ]
- [ ]
- [ ]
- [ ]
- [ ]
- [ ]
- [ ]
- [ ]
- [ ]
- [ ]
- [ ]

Emergency:

Parents:

Where we'll be:

Cell Phone:

Emergency

Phone #:

Child 1

Allergies

Child 2

Allergies

Child 3

Allergies

Child 4

Allergies

Meals:

No No:

Snacks:

Rules:

Bedtime:

Notes:

Babysitter Info

Emergency:

Parents:

Where we'll be:

Cell Phone:

Emergency

Phone #:

Child 1

Allergies

Child 2

Allergies

Child 3

Allergies

Child 4

Allergies

To Do:

- [ ]
- [ ]
- [ ]
- [ ]
- [ ]
- [ ]
- [ ]
- [ ]
- [ ]
- [ ]
- [ ]
- [ ]

Meals:

No No:

Snacks:

Rules:

Bedtime:

Notes:

Birthday Reminders

January

February

March

April

May

June

Birthday Reminders

July

August

September

October

November

December

Birthday Reminders

January

February

March

April

May

June

Birthday Reminders

July

August

September

October

November

December

Milage Tracker

MAKE:		MODEL:		YEAR:
DATE:	ODOMETER: START | END		TOTAL:	DESTINATION / PURPOSE:

Milage Tracker

MAKE:		MODEL:		YEAR:
DATE:	ODOMETER: START | END		TOTAL:	DESTINATION / PURPOSE:

Milage Tracker

MAKE:		MODEL:		YEAR:
DATE:	ODOMETER: START | END		TOTAL:	DESTINATION / PURPOSE:

Milage Tracker

MAKE:		MODEL:		YEAR:
DATE:	ODOMETER: START | END		TOTAL:	DESTINATION / PURPOSE:

Tax Info

Name ______________________________

Financial Year ________________

☐

☐

☐

☐

☐

☐

☐

☐

☐

☐

☐

☐

☐

☐

☐

☐

☐

☐

☐

☐

☐

Tax Info

Name ______________________________

Financial Year ______________

- ☐
- ☐
- ☐
- ☐
- ☐
- ☐
- ☐
- ☐
- ☐
- ☐
- ☐
- ☐
- ☐
- ☐
- ☐
- ☐
- ☐
- ☐
- ☐
- ☐
- ☐

Tax Info

Name ______________________________

Financial Year ________________

- [ ]
- [ ]
- [ ]
- [ ]
- [ ]
- [ ]
- [ ]
- [ ]
- [ ]
- [ ]
- [ ]
- [ ]
- [ ]
- [ ]
- [ ]
- [ ]
- [ ]
- [ ]
- [ ]
- [ ]
- [ ]

Tax Info

Name ______________________________

Financial Year ______________

- ☐ ______________________________
- ☐ ______________________________
- ☐ ______________________________
- ☐ ______________________________
- ☐ ______________________________
- ☐ ______________________________
- ☐ ______________________________
- ☐ ______________________________
- ☐ ______________________________
- ☐ ______________________________
- ☐ ______________________________
- ☐ ______________________________
- ☐ ______________________________
- ☐ ______________________________
- ☐ ______________________________
- ☐ ______________________________
- ☐ ______________________________
- ☐ ______________________________
- ☐ ______________________________
- ☐ ______________________________
- ☐ ______________________________

Tax Checklist

Name ______________________________

Financial Year ______________

- ☐ Tax ID / social security number/ tax file number: ______________
- ☐ Previous year's tax statements

INCOME

☐ Day Job	☐ ______________
☐ Bank account details	☐ ______________
☐ Bank statements	☐ ______________
☐ Dividends on investments	☐ ______________
☐ Business income	☐ ______________
☐ Blog income	☐ ______________
☐ Foreign income	☐ ______________
☐ Investment property income	☐ ______________

EXPENSES

☐ Day Job	☐ ______________
☐ Business	☐ ______________
☐ Blog	☐ ______________
☐ Investment property	☐ ______________
☐ Charity	☐ ______________
☐ Medical	☐ ______________
☐ Interest paid on loans	☐ ______________
☐ Child /Children related expenses	☐ ______________

Tax Checklist

Name ______________________________

Financial Year ______________

☐ Tax ID / social security number/ tax file number: ______________

☐ Previous year's tax statements

INCOME

☐ Day Job ☐ ______________

☐ Bank account details ☐ ______________

☐ Bank statements ☐ ______________

☐ Dividends on investments ☐ ______________

☐ Business income ☐ ______________

☐ Blog income ☐ ______________

☐ Foreign income ☐ ______________

☐ Investment property income ☐ ______________

EXPENSES

☐ Day Job ☐ ______________

☐ Business ☐ ______________

☐ Blog ☐ ______________

☐ Investment property ☐ ______________

☐ Charity ☐ ______________

☐ Medical ☐ ______________

☐ Interest paid on loans ☐ ______________

☐ Child /Children related expenses ☐ ______________

Tax Checklist

Name ______________________________

Financial Year ______________

- ☐ Tax ID / social security number/ tax file number: ______________
- ☐ Previous year's tax statements

INCOME

☐ Day Job	☐ ______________
☐ Bank account details	☐ ______________
☐ Bank statements	☐ ______________
☐ Dividends on investments	☐ ______________
☐ Business income	☐ ______________
☐ Blog income	☐ ______________
☐ Foreign income	☐ ______________
☐ Investment property income	☐ ______________

EXPENSES

☐ Day Job	☐ ______________
☐ Business	☐ ______________
☐ Blog	☐ ______________
☐ Investment property	☐ ______________
☐ Charity	☐ ______________
☐ Medical	☐ ______________
☐ Interest paid on loans	☐ ______________
☐ Child /Children related expenses	☐ ______________

Tax Checklist

Name ________________________________

Financial Year ______________

- ☐ Tax ID / social security number/ tax file number: ______________
- ☐ Previous year's tax statements

INCOME

- ☐ Day Job ☐ ______________
- ☐ Bank account details ☐ ______________
- ☐ Bank statements ☐ ______________
- ☐ Dividends on investments ☐ ______________
- ☐ Business income ☐ ______________
- ☐ Blog income ☐ ______________
- ☐ Foreign income ☐ ______________
- ☐ Investment property income ☐ ______________

EXPENSES

- ☐ Day Job ☐ ______________
- ☐ Business ☐ ______________
- ☐ Blog ☐ ______________
- ☐ Investment property ☐ ______________
- ☐ Charity ☐ ______________
- ☐ Medical ☐ ______________
- ☐ Interest paid on loans ☐ ______________
- ☐ Child /Children related expenses ☐ ______________

Embracing the Peace Within

By Dr. Jennifer Jones Bryant

Practice mindfulness for self-care and self-awareness. Part of practicing self-care is building a relationship with yourself. Your first step is to become aware and begin to develop a vocabulary for how you're feeling. Be fair to yourself, and not judge yourself harshly and believe negative stories about yourself. Letting go of the need to judge is very powerful. It creates space for the feelings to be present without creating negative around them. When you begin to give yourself the love and unconditional acceptance you seek, you will be less concerned with what others think and freer to make choices that are in alignment with what you genuinely want.

Finding Purpose For Alignment

If you can tune into your purpose and really align with it, setting goals so that your vision is an expression of that purpose, then life flows much more easily. Jack Canfield

Initiate your first steps to launch your purpose by focusing on your short and long-term goals. Goal setting gives you something tangible to work towards daily. Make sure your progress is documented somewhere so you can reflect on them, and don't forget to celebrate your wins. Purpose-driven mindsets involve setting Specific, Measurable, Attainable, Result-Oriented, and Timely goals. Goal setting is a great way to own your growth journey. Devotions, visualization, planning, focus, and hard work are all necessary for achieving goals.

Inspirational Quote

"With every act of self-care your authentic self gets stronger, and the critical, fearful mind gets weaker. Every act of self-care is a powerful declaration: I am on my side, I am on my side, each day I am more and more on my own side."
-- Susan Weiss Berry

Affirmations

My self-care is a priority.
I will show myself grace and mercy.
I will start my day with prayer or meditation,
cultivate gratitude, foster forgiveness,
and commit to positive affirmations.

I don't give up on my happiness and growth. I write down the goals and steps needed to manifest my goals. My written goals are helping me to achieve my life's purpose. I believe in myself and my ability to reach my goals.

Born For This

By Christina Alva

Inspirational Quote

If you can dream it, you can do it.
- Walt Disney

Scripture

I can do all things through Christ Jesus,
who strengthens me.
- Philippians 4:13

Journal Questions

1. Sometimes when you share your dreams with others who don't have the same mindset as you, it can be discouraging. It's because they can't see your vision. They may laugh at you or make you feel silly for thinking big. You have to be careful with who you share your dreams. God gave you the vision, not them. Don't be afraid to claim your dreams. **What is the biggest dream you have ever had?**

2. Nobody will live forever. **When you think about your children and what kind of an inheritance you want to leave them, what does that look like? Do you just want to leave the money in the bank to pay off their bills? Or how about a house that they could use or sell? Think bigger. If you could leave a legacy for your children, what would it be?**

3. If you are thinking of starting a business, you might be stuck on what type of business to start. Try starting by first identifying your passions what you like to do. When thinking about your passions and the things you love to do, it can be difficult to pinpoint that one thing. It is easy to think about all the many things you like to do. **What is that one passion, that one thing that brings you joy? Put in another way, if money was not an issue, what would your life look like today? What would you be doing?**

4. Another way to pick a business is to think about your purpose. **Another way to put it is if you had to help 100 people, in what way would you help them?**

Visionista

By Phyllis Hunter

Dear Woman CEO**,** You are embarking on an incredible journey. It won't be easy, but if you stick with it, it will be worth it. God gave you an incredible gift, the gift of vision. On this journey, you will encounter many who will not understand your vision and some who will. Remember that the vision wasn't given to them, it was given to you, and it is up to you to see it through. **You have a purpose, and God has a plan for you to prosper and not harm you. A plan for hope and a future. (Jeremiah 29:11)**

I first started my mompreneur journey in 2012 when I returned home from a military assignment. I was broken, facing a divorce, and learning to be a single parent, not to mention my bank account was empty. The only work experience I had was training soldiers, combat, and logistics. So I tested the waters with different Network Marketing companies. Some I made money and some not so much. I learned the principles of sales, personal development, and leverage. Those fundamental principles helped me create the level of success I have today.

After many years of trial and error, I finally became my boss. I had a great mentor who taught me how to form an LLC; like me, she too was a mompreneur and had lettered success for her family. My company's vision was to inspire others to be and do great things as God created us. I wanted to inspire my children to be great, and I knew it had to start with me showing them how. I consulted for daycare to generate income and learned to print t-shirts on the side. When the pandemic first took place in late 2019/early 2020, I took my t-shirt business full time. Printing on t-shirts and masks encouraged people, but I wouldn't say it inspired them. It was a way to generate income for me, my children, and my company. You will find you need capital to fund your business during your journey. I didn't want to take out a loan, and if you're like me, you probably don't want to either. So while figuring out my game plan for my business, I had to do things that would create the funds necessary to keep the business afloat. I continued to work at the daycare, driving food services, and became a licensed insurance agent. There is no shame in this process. Every entrepreneur faces this moment where cash flow is an issue. However, if you have a foundational source of income, it helps keep you afloat so that you don't financially drown.

It wasn't until I met a gentleman who would soon inspire me to reinvent myself. There are several phases of business, and in each phase, you will need to reinvent yourself to become the woman God has created you to be. I went from being the woman who produced to the woman who teaches. I began teaching small business owners to market their brands by using my products. I printed their logos and branded their merchandise on various products like clothing and accessories. I learned that I could inspire small business owners by bringing the vision of their brand to life while on an affordable budget. I learned that I could increase revenue by providing professional merchandise at a wholesale price and teaching other entrepreneurs the power of branding through merchandise. At that moment, I could see my company's vision come to life. That same gentleman also introduced me to a young woman who would then show me other ways I could inspire people, resulting in a book being published and more projects to come in the future. That book teaches entrepreneurs how to turn their hobby into a business, the same way I had done. Because of these influential partnerships, my company has been elevated to new levels and will continue to thrive. And you, Woman CEO, have the power to do the same thing. Since deciding to take my business full time, I have been overwhelmingly blessed with many opportunities to rise in the way God has proposed. It has been a fantastic journey thus far, and I have the utmost faith it will continue to be. I know in my heart of hearts that if you continue to run this race, your journey will be blessed. **The race is not given to the swift nor the strong but to the one who endures until the end. (Ecclesiastes 9:11)**

If I knew back then what I know now, it wouldn't have taken so long to get to where I am today. So if I could give you some advice to help you progress and succeed, I would say personal development and a mentor will be your best friend. A mentor or coach will help guide you in the direction you want to go. They become an accountability partner to assist you in your success. Personal development will push you through the tough times and keep you humble during the successes. Personal development will enhance your mind, heart, and spirit and lead you through the creative process. As entrepreneurs, we are the visionaries, and as visionaries, it is up to us to see that this God-given vision comes to fruition. A mentor will guide you to the proper personal development when you need it the most.

Leverage will open doors to opportunities you never thought possible. God gave you a gift to operate in, and those who seek entrepreneurship as a way to operate in that gift often get paid to do so. There's nothing wrong with getting paid for your gift. However, you cannot do it on your own, so it is essential to leverage others. By leveraging those who can help you on this journey, you can accomplish more in a shorter time frame. For example, I did not know much about properly using sales techniques, so I had to learn. I leveraged a sales professional who taught me what I needed to know. If I had the capital at that time, I would have just hired a sales professional to run the sales department of my business. Still, I didn't have the capital, so I leveraged them for their knowledge and was able to apply their teachings instead. If you have the opportunity to either hire or learn from someone who could do what you couldn't, I recommend leveraging them for their talent or gift.

I'd also tell you to lead with the vision in mind. You are the one with the dream, and the passion for that dream also comes from you. When you know where you want to go with your business, you will continue to push through and be intentional in the moves you make regarding your business. Be very clear on your vision and where you are going. Write the vision down and make it as simple and straightforward as possible so that you may see it every day and run towards your goals. (Habakkuk 2:2) God will provide the how when you are clear on where you are going. He will send mentors and coaches to guide you and the leverage you need to accomplish the mission.

And finally, the last key piece of advice I can give you is to take action now! Now faith is the substance of things hoped for and the evidence of things not seen. (Hebrews 11:1) God calls us to have faith. Faith is a verb. It means action. To have faith is to take action. God calls us to take action, not just any kind of action but NOW ACTION. We hope for a fantastic outcome when we start our business. We hope to succeed. We even hope for a successful life with an incredible lifestyle, but we must take action for us to have that. Not a year from now or ten years from now action, but now action.

Action is the proof of your faith. If you say you believe you can have the desired life you want, then why aren't you taking steps to make it come alive? Action is the evidence of your faith. Action is what makes your vision come to fruition. Action is the manifestation of your thoughts. So if you are a woman of faith, you are a woman of action, **for it is impossible to please God without faith (Hebrews 11:6).** Therefore it is impossible to please God without faith in action. So go out there and take action. It is your destiny for your vision to come to pass; as it is in heaven, so shall it be here on earth. I pray this message finds you well along your journey. Woman CEO, you are created for greatness, and greatness is created for you. It will take some work, but anything worth having is worth fighting for. I believe in you, mompreneur; now believe in yourself.

Dare to Dream Exponentially

By Lakeisa Arrington

Dare to Dream Again! Mompreneurs are extraordinary individuals who shape and mold our very existence. We are complex, unique, strong, powerful, brilliant, fearfully and wonderfully made curvaceous beings. We bring home the bacon, fry it up in the pan, sort the laundry, mop the floor, bathe the kids, check the homework, pray over the kids, take care of the husband, walk the dog, feed the goldfish, then retire for the night sometime after midnight. We rise early in the morning only to repeat the process time and time again. Mothers spend so much time doing everything for everybody that we forget what matters the most, ourselves.

Mom, I spent so much time trying to be everything for everybody that I forgot what I was created to be. I forgot how to spend time with "me." I forgot how to love on "me." I forgot about the other phenomenal sides of "me." I forgot about the gifts and talents that were inside of "me". I forgot about the little eight year old that had a DREAM! At the age of eight, I wanted to create. I wanted to design. I wanted to connect people. My parents would purchase mini architectural boxed sets that allowed me to build an entire city. My dad and I spent hours building ice cream parlors, gas stations and other buildings that fit perfectly on his full size race car set that he stored underneath the couch. My dream was to be an architect.

Well, that was one of my dreams. I also wanted to become a fashion designer. I had a wonderful neighbor that lived on the third floor. Her name was Ms. Maxine; and Ms. Maxine was a seamstress that gave me all of her leftover fabric and taught me how to sew. I was beyond ecstatic. I would lay on the floor and use markers to record my measurements to the best of my ability. The next day I would have a hand sewn"Lakeisa McCain" original. My parents believed in my creative vision and purchased drafting paper and tools to assist me in creating my designer's originals.

My dream did not end there. I ran lemonade stands, cookie stands and sold baked goods. I even hosted weekly movie nights. I charged a fee for entry, purchased candy from the neighborhood ice cream truck then showed movies using my "Give a Show" projector. My dream was to be a business owner. My dreams were limitless. The desires of my heart as a child turned into dreams I could design and I was able to do exactly what I loved. Now is the time for you to dream again. Take a well deserved self care day and spend time with the little girl inside of you that had limitless dreams.

Dare to Dream Big! Somewhere along the line the limitless dreams I had as a little girl started to fade. Life happened; who knew? My family dynamics changed. My interests changed. I entered middle school and started break dancing. I temporarily discovered a new dream. I wanted to be a break dancer; just like the ones I saw in the movie, Breaking 2: Electric Boogaloo. Don't judge me. I forgot about those dreams that ignited the flame in my belly as a little girl. In high school the dream to be a famous fashion designer surfaced once again and I was heading to New York to study fashion at F. I. T; the one and only Fashion Institute of Technology. Unfortunately, that Big Dream fizzled because I was too afraid to leave home.

2 Timothy 1:7 Reminds us that God has not given us the spirit of fear, but of power, love and of instruction.

Now why didn't I know that scripture in High School. I stayed home sewing clothes for myself during my early years of college while also doing hair. I may have forgotten the dynamic dreams of my eight year old self, but God never did. That entrepreneurial spirit that was birthed in me stayed with me. Although I did not attend F.I.T, I received hands-on experience in the world of Fashion as an employee at Neiman Marcus in Washington, DC. I learned so much about the insides of the fashion world from a retail perspective. I studied the designers, built relationships with buyers, became a personal shopper and worked my way up to an assistant manager. I would tell my coworkers that one day they would see my designs in boutiques around the world.

In 2012 items from my children's clothing line were featured in the display window and sold at "The Purple Goose." The Purple Goose is a children's boutique that has been in business for almost 30 years. They are located in Alexandria, Va. One year later, pieces from my children's clothing line were also featured in the display window and sold at "Yogaso " children's boutique in North Bethesda. God promises to give you the desires of your heart. I forgot about the dreams of my eight year old self; but God did not. He is faithful. I ran into a friend 3 years ago that worked with me at Neiman Marcus. She said, "Lakeisa, I follow you on Instagram and I want you to know that I am so proud of you. Do you remember the time when you said, 'One day I would own a children's boutique and my clothes would be in stores everywhere'"? I did not remember until she reminded me. As a mompreneur I learned to dream God size dreams. I learned to show up consistently. I desire to leave a legacy for children and my children's children. Most importantly, I understand my "Why!" My "Why" keeps me going. My "Why" keeps me encouraged. My "Why" helps me stay the course.

Dare to set Boundaries! Your dream was given to you. Therefore, everyone won't always understand your dream. They may not even support your dream. Some may even despise your dream. Nevertheless, what God has for you is for you and your dream is so much larger than you. My eight year old self had dreams of being a business owner, designer and human connector. If she only knew that our journey would include becoming a mom, wife, grandmother, minister, designer, coach and consultant with 20 plus years in the Human Resource arena, and 15 plus years as a mentor to teenagers, perhaps she would have taught other kids how to dream exponentially. I am proud of my journey, the good, the bad and the ugly. Today I am the proud owner of "The Experience by LA " a purpose pusher brand that purposely pushes men and women into designing their dreams while growing professionally, personally and spiritually. I teach women how to connect their passion to their purpose based on divine promises that lead to prosperity in every area of their life. I am also the creator behind "Naya's Closet" an apparel brand that creates custom couture and one of a kind fashion for your unique curves.

I am able to own my greatness and dream exponentially because I learned to set boundaries. I shared my dreams with my family. I involved my children and my spouse in the process. I learned that "No" is a complete sentence and that my "No" had power. The more I found the courage to say "No" the more I was able to say "Yes" to things connected to my dreams. I learned to love myself unconditionally; therefore, self care was no longer optional. I invested in myself and did not ask permission to become the best version of myself. I hired a coach to help me maneuver through obstacles that kept me from manifesting my dreams. I established a daily gratitude routine. I identified people, places and things that kept me emotionally bound and distracted from my dreams. Being intentional and strategic when setting boundaries was a game changer for me.

Mom, I believe in you. I admonish you to Dream beyond the galaxy. Speak your dreams daily, write your dreams day and night and keep them in front of you. I want you to be specific and be strategic. Dream books, dream boards or a dream wall can help you with visualization. Remember to focus on your "WHY;" your Why is connected to your purpose. Maintain an attitude of gratitude by praying about everything and worrying about nothing. Practice affirmation meditations because we become what we think. Hire a mentor or a coach because the word reminds us to seek wise counsel. Believe in yourself, believe in your dream, believe that God has an extraordinary expected end with your name on it. Last but not least, now is the time to take action; for Faith without works is dead. See you on the other side of endless possibilities and exponential dreams!

Journal Questions

1. What boundaries will you set?
2. What dreams have you forgotten?
3. What dreams do you need to grant yourself permission to dream again?

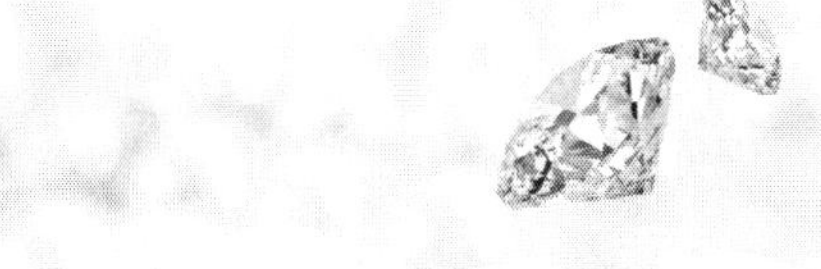

Passion, Perils and Purpose:
The Evolution of the Mom CEO

By Constance Woulard

Scripture

For I know the plans I have for you, saith the Lord.
Plans to prosper you and not to harm you.
Plans to give you hope and a future.
- Jeremiah 29:11:

Affirmation

My purpose in life is preordained through the Lord.

This purpose was assigned yet, while I was being formed in my mother's womb. The divine confirmation is that I am wonderfully and perfectly designed to do the work to edify His Kingdom. I will not fail. He has bestowed unto me the necessary tools to be successful in this life. It is my duty to be obedient and walk boldly into my divine purpose. He has my back, my front, my sides, and my flank. He protects and guides me throughout this journey. Failure is not an option. Opportunities trump obstacles. My relationship with God is one of want and not need. He wants me as His daughter.

He supplies my every need.

Journal Questions

1. What is your divine purpose?
2. How has this been affirmed in your spiritual and physical life?
3. What confirmation has been provided to you that you are truly living in your divine purpose.

Managing Mompreneur Work Life Balance

By Amber Mabry

Scriptures

"But seek ye first the kingdom of God, and his righteousness; and all these things shall be added unto you."
Matthew 6:33 KJV

"Rejoice always, pray continually, give thanks in all circumstances; for this is God's will for you in Christ Jesus."
1 Thessalonians 5:16-18 NIV

Inspirational Quote:

"LIVE OUT LOUD!"

Affirmation

I can *do whatever I set my mind to do.*

I will *give myself grace today.*

I believe *I was born with purpose to create impact and change in the world around me.*

I will stand up *on the stage of my life and live unapologetically... because I am a child of God.*

Journal Questions

1. Why am I / do I want to be an entrepreneur?
2. How can I organize my life so that I can best manage my home and business life?
3. What 3-5 words represent the type of legacy I hope to leave for my children? Why?
4. What areas of my life can I delegate to be more present at home? (Examples: meal prep, grocery delivery, laundry services, hired virtual assistant, etc.)
5. What will I do to ensure I make time for personal self-care every week/month?
6. What is my definition of success?

Just Figure it Out

By Teri Garrett

Not once in the Bible does It say Worry about it, Stress over it, or figure it out. AHHHHHHHHHH!!!!

But over and over, it clearly says, "TRUST GOD."

Many of you start your day by Laying in bed just as I do.

This morning at 5:48 a.m., my mind began to race. I thought about what to pay first and what emails I needed to prioritize and schedule the building inspection for the daycare center. Thinking if we should get more clients for the home care agency, or leave it be. We barely have staff to cover the clients we have now. When can I go to the gym? OMG, back to what bills to pay, plus the extra things that need to be paid to help my brand to expand. Hmm, I think I can ask my best friend if I can borrow the funds until I get my income tax back? My mind began to race as if I was going Into panic mode; I had to talk myself into calming down. "Get up, Teri, and start your day." I got up to let the dog out and fed her. I asked myself, "why do you do this all the time? Just worrying and stressing."

Walk by Faith, Not by Sight...

Remember, He (God) has you covered. Has He (God) failed you yet? Is he not always on time?

As moms, there is always something to stress over or worry about.

After letting the dog back in, I waited for the children to enter the daycare. I did a routine check of my emails and bank accounts. I noticed extra funding in the daycare account; I checked it and instantly began smiling and giving praises! I had to look at my man upstairs and tell him, "Ok, God; I get it, I get it! If I'm going to TRUST you, I have to TRUST you!" Oh, not to mention we lost a client, but only to gain a client within 5 minutes, only one daycare child left at 4 p.m. on a Friday!!!! That only means I will make it to the gym by 6.... I must say today is a good day!

Just like my day worked out with the help of God, so will yours!

Journal Questions

1. Am I going to worry, or am I going to pray, activate my faith and works?
2. What things do you need to do today? (Write a list hour by hour.)
3. Ask yourself how I can prioritize my day not to seem so overwhelming?
4. How can I delegate some tasks to my staff?

   (Maybe you are just starting and don't have a staff.)
5. Ask yourself what task I can get the children or my spouse to help me with?
6. Do you have the resources to hire someone to help me?

It's The Mom in Me

By Renee Ambush

"I just want to tell the truth... I just want to tell the truth! You're so fly, you're... everybody round you trying to figure out why...What they don't know is when I go home and get behind closed door and man I hit the floor. What they can't see is when I am on my knees! GOD!!!!"

Mompreneur takes being relentlessness. It takes sacrifice and scutiny. Its having to have time management and even money management. Yet, with all this one of the biggest attribute to have as a Mompreneur is Understanding of Self. The way we see ourselves is the way we show up as Mompreneur. For example, I struggled with self worth and struggled with placing value on what I provided for others. I didnt see my accomplishments and excellence and it hindered me from operating in my GOD given PURPOSE with confidence.

Be ye transformed by the Renewal of your mind. - Romans 12:2

Once identifying that I was settling and accepting of less began my relentless in the journey to self. I changed my thoughts about myself. I activated GODfidence! It was my journey that strengthen my ability to help others overcome. My mistakes became my message that ultimately became my miracles.

There will come a time when love will blow your mind and everything you'll look for you'll find (take a look inside). Thre will be a time that everything will shine so bright it makes you color blind. If I gave you diamonds and pearls; would you be a happy boy or a girl? If I could I would give you the world. All I can do is just offer you my love. In my love I offer you these five points on navigating a successful road in Mompreneurship.

Affirmations

* Know that GOD has made you AMAZING and EQUIPPED you with everything pertaining to live and Godliness.

* You have what it takes to be successful.

* Your past nor your mistakes define you and shall it be a final destination to fail.

* With every step you take no matter how small, Celebrate you.

* Continually recite and believe positive affirmations.

Journal Questions

1. What thoughts am I holding on to that is hindering my success?
2. How do I see me and is that how I believe GOD sees me?
3. If I had everything needed to be successful what would I succeed in?

I have done and continually do the work in me to assist you in become the greatest you. Because where you are is not where you ought to be; step out of the realm of self incarceration and be free. Time to get OUT THA BOX. www.RebirthofRenee.com

Third Generation Mompreneur

By Alonda Brooks

For I know the plans I have for you, declares the lord, plans to prosper you and not harm you, plans to give you a hope and a future. - Jeremiah 29:11 KJV

Listen I do not know about you, but this scripture is one of my favorites.

I can remember being lost after my divorce and try to make my way back to someone I recognized and all I could think about was all the visions and plans I had before I got lost in marriage, I wanted more than anything to get back to my ambitious self. What I found peace in was knowing that all though life had changed my path, I also knew that I served a God who had designed my purpose before I knew myself and that he already had made provisions for all bumps and left turns I would take on my path . God is the greatest mathematician ever he had every variable figured out ahead of time. I challenge you to find peace and joy and to denounce worrying about your purpose. God already has it worked out for you and your purpose will emerge out of your pain. I know things have been scary and an uncertain since the pandemic but I believe the best is yet to come for you! God has so much stored up for us in the store house. So take this next year purposefully and intentionally by force and become! Say today I will walk in my purpose because I am sure that I have one. I will not let my past be my fear of moving forward in my purpose.

To everything there is a season, and a time to every purpose under the heaven... - Ecclesiastes 3:1

Have you been operating in your purpose, but it seems like there just hasn't been much fruit to match your labor?

Allow me to reassure you a lot of God's greatest thing are produce under pressure and often times with very little visibility to the naked eye for example a diamond is by far the most revered stone yup you guessed it made under pressure. A pearl made at the bottom of the sea hidden inside of a shell starting from a mere grain of sand however you also know made under pressure. Everyone loves a great sweet potatoes pie or a nice, candied yam on holidays. What if I told you that a sweet potatoes is planted in an unusual season below ground with no evidence that it is down below the soil. You simple must know its season to harvest and remember where you planted it, but we walk on the ground yes, I think you are getting it made under pressure. Here is the point often we measure the success of our purpose based on the fruit that others lives bare not considering that our fruit is simply an invisible harvest and its not yet time for our crop to come in. I encourage you never doubt your purpose because there is no tree or flower blooming signifying your harvest. Keep in mind to everything there is a season and a time for everything. God will use your becoming as a testimony in due season.

Affirm to yourself: I will use every test as a builder of my testimony."
I will stand in the conviction of my truth.

This is the purpose that is purposed upon the whole earth: and this is the hand that is stretched out upon all the nations. - Isaiah 14:26

If you are a listener of my show, i Am Becoming then you are familiar with my quote: *Do not do anything for man's approval but do everything with man in mind.* What this means is we are all a part of the circle of life so ultimately me being in alignment with my purpose and doing my part will affect others. I challenge you if you have not been walking in your purpose boldly do it and do it now. The pandemic has taught us that time waits for no man and that everything that we need to do our part in this large world is already inside of us and our life experiences only awaken us to our capacity to give back and do our part to inspire ,uplift, and give charity. There is such a sense of purpose when you are operating in your purpose often times people are searching to know what their purpose is .I say you will find your purpose in the purest most active part of your heart the part where your joy lives. Your purpose will be the activities that makes your heart feel like it will beat out of its chest you will feel like you had the best breath of fresh air after walking in your purpose. I encourage you to not over think it is usually not buried that deep. I also encourage to pour out as much of it as you can on this world leave here empty withholding nothing. Have you ever heard the old song at a funeral let the works that I have done speak for me? Live on purpose be blessed. *Say with me I believe my purpose will lead me to all that God has for me in abundance.*

Journal Questions

1. How will I start investing in my purpose?
2. Will I pay with time, energy or financial resources first?
3. What in your past have you allowed to stand in the way of fulfilling your purpose personally ?
4. What from your past has been hindering your professional growth ?
5. What seeds will you plant for your children and their children's children?
6. What systems do you need to create for yourself care, children, and business to prosper fully ?
7. What kind of community do I need to create for myself and family to walk boldly in my purpose?

More is Caught Than Taught

By Carolyn Jones

Inspirational Quote:

"Your children would rather join you than just watch you – let them."

Scriptures

And then God answered: "Write this. Write what you see. Write it out in big block letters so that it can be read on the run. This vision-message is a witness pointing to what's coming. It aches for the coming—it can hardly wait! And it doesn't lie. If it seems slow in coming, wait. It's on its way. It will come right on time. Habakkuk 2:2-3 [MSG]

Journal Questions

1. What are some small tasks that you can give your children to do to help in your business?

2. How can you structure their pay to show them how to monetize their contributions (i.e. a percentage of proceeds, hourly pay, wages vs allowance, etc.)?

3. How can you reward them by mentioning them in your success testimony?

Now . . . do it and watch the win win for all – just watch . . . "if it seems slow in coming, wait. It's on its way. It WILL come right on time." I promise.

Jewels to Become A Successful Mompreneur

By Tara Omotosho

You have been Fearfully and Wonderfully Made! - Psalm 139:14

Look in You! God has already equipped you. You have talent. You have the confidence you need. You are smart enough. You have the skills. You have the strength you need. You are good enough. Don't discount yourself!

1. What can you do to create the right balance for your life?

Evaluate your time and determine when you will work on your dreams. Have those conversations with those family members and friends who are willing to support you.

"Today I am going to create the right balance for my life."

2. Create your strong drive statement and set your goals.

Ask yourself, "What is driving me to do this business?"
Ask yourself, "I must do this because, what?"

Write this statement or declaration down.

Setting Goals:
Think about what you want to achieve in the first 3 months, the next 6 months and then the first year and write these down as realistic goals. Be as specific as possible and add monetary values (the income your business will generate) and specific milestones you want to achieve (such as work with specific clients or brands).

3 Month Goals:

6 Month Goals:

My 1 year in business goal:

3. Make sure you write down a "to do" list every day. Write it on paper so it is visible before you and you can cross things out once they are completed.

4. Continue to learn as you earn. Ask yourself every day what new things can I learn today? What new seminars or courses will assist me in getting further in my business? Write those courses here:

5. Collaborate and Outsource. Ask yourself, who can I collaborate with? Who can I outsource this task to? Make a list of key resource people and their skills:

Contact Information:

Name: ______________________________

Skill: ______________________________

Contact Information:

Name: ______________________________

Skill: ______________________________

Contact Information:

Name: ______________________________

Skill: ______________________________

Contact Information:

Name: ______________________________

Skill: ______________________________

Contact Information:

Name: ______________________________

Skill: ______________________________

A Proverbs Womenpreneur

By Donna Chang

Scriptures

Your gifts will make room for you and bring you before great men! - Proverbs 18:16

I honestly didn't know that the gift of my grandmother's talent being taught to me at such a young age would bring me before great men. I had the honor of doing celebrity weddings. For a long time, the gift sustained my family's supplemental needs.

The Lord is my shepherd; I shall not want. He maketh me to lie down in green pastures: He leadeth me beside the still waters. - Psalms 23

For the Lord, thy God has given you the POWER to create wealth so that He may establish His covenant! - Deut 8:18

Speak those things that are not as though they were. - Romans 4:17

Continue to speak over your current circumstances as if they are already working out for your good. Speak and walk as a success. I wish you nothing but success and endless positive possibilities.

Journal Questions

1. What gift and talents are you sitting on to help you make a sustainable income to support your family or your dreams and goals?
2. What do you fear about being or becoming a successful entrepreneur?

Conquering Mompreneurship

By Christina Ivette

Inspirational Quote

"Own Your Tomorrow"
- Myrna Roman

Own your tomorrow sis! Own your future boss self. Own your actions. Own your position in this chain. Own your journey. You are an amazing woman, amazing mother, amazing business owner. The things you do today will shape your tomorrow. So keep moving forward daily to accomplish all your goals. Your goals will change the trajectory of your life. Your life is a direct correlation of your actions. So continue being one of the greats. Because you are creating a legacy and you too will go down in history.

Affirmations

Affirmation 1: **I am a phenomenal mother**

Affirmation 2: **I am a boss scaling my business**

Affirmation 3: **I am creating generational wealth**

Journal Questions

1. Have you ever thought about opening up a business for your child?
2. Did you know you can pay your child as an employee in your business?
3. What type of legacy are you going to leave behind?

My Sister Keeper

By Nadia Monsano

Inspirational Quote

"The most beautiful thing a woman can wear is her confidence."

Journal Questions

1. What are some things that you can do in order to show up confident in your business?
2. What is the next level to your business? Are you ready?
3. Why did you start your business and are you nurturing your business for success and to pass it along to the next generation?

Faith Filled And Fearless

By Jordan Pogue

"Now faith is the substance of things hoped for, the evidence of things not seen." - Hebrews 11:1

You're the only one who can do what God has called you to do! You're the only one who can tell your testimony and no one else! Eunoia Boutique started off as a business idea that popped into my head during a Bible study session. God helped my dream come to pass, but just because it's a God driven business doesn't mean it will be easy! This business, although it's a baby, has encountered plenty of battles from the spirits of fear, doubt and anxiety, but God helped me contend with it all! Being called to do something can seem scary when you don't see yourself the same way God sees you. Having faith means not seeing things move in the natural but to rely on knowing that God has already finished it in the supernatural! This walk of faith was never guaranteed to be easy but God did promise to be with you every step of the way.

Journal Questions

1. Do you consult God for all things that you need?
2. Even if God doesn't deliver His promise on time will you have faith to know that it will come in His timing?
3. Can you allow your faith to be louder then the doubt and anxiety that you may face?

It's Our Season

By Meighan Cole

Mommiepreneur,
I am speaking to the woman I see who is just like me standing in a mirror, taking a million photos to get one right—having a bad hair day, trying to let her hair down, trying to tackle one child at a time and divide her time equally while loving and caring for her. I want that woman to know that I acknowledge her, I commend her, I may not know her- struggle, but I want her to know that I see her!

Mark 9:23 "ALL things are possible to him that believes!"
We are not settling or playing it small!
We are Capable of Winning.

Queens, Diamonds in a Rough, pressure making it is time that we RISE UP. It is not time for us to walk with our heads hung low, a frown on our faces. Queen, it is time to ARISE to be the Queens we are called to be doing it unapologetically and without the need of anyone's permission. If GOD said, we could have a life of abundance, blessings, love, joy, and happiness. So why should we doubt it? Why don't we grasp ahold of his life for us? The one that he promised us, knowing that what God has for us is for us, it is time that we believe in his promises.

No longer will we allow our vision, hopes, and dreams to fall away like a thief in the night. We must take our power back, lift our heads and RISE to the occasion and the present opportunities. If God puts it in our path, it means it is attainable and nothing that we cannot concur or have when he is in the mix. It is time that we manifest the life that we deserve and stop playing it small. It is time to celebrate our wins, practice loving ourselves more and hold ourselves accountable for the life we want to live.

Pause for a moment and tell yourself I am worthy, I got this, and there is absolutely nothing in this world that I cannot have or do! The life that you want to live and have is an answer away. It is in your thoughts, prayers, and daily manifestations. There is nothing wrong with manifesting the life you want to live. Don't let small minds tell you different because they cannot comprehend what your giant GOD will do in and through you.

"I remember growing up in foster care being told that I was just a number or would be just like others and fail. "My exact reply was no; I am not. I will rise above and beat the odds and be everything that GOD said I would be watching my smoke. Today I still have more work to do. I am always a work in progress. I have to stop and thank God for how far I have come." Queen, take a moment and count your blessings, sometimes count them twice, and thank GOD for your growth, his favor, and his protection over your life.

Continue to be encouraged. Start praising him, Queen, and claim that everything attached to you will WIN. Your children, family, finances, relationships, dreams, and visions know that you are only one step, one door opening away from your winning season. Unleash the woman in you that GOD created within you; know that you are more than capable of winning no matter where you are today. It would help if you believed that you do not have to settle, that it is your season to reap what you have sown. It would help if you believed more than anyone that it was your season. You may believe that you have only sown a tiny seed, BUT know that GOD is a BIG GOD and tiny seeds are a sacrifice that reaps a BIG HARVEST.

Mommiepreneur, do not put another dream on hold; don't bury another gift deep down on your inside. It is time to Rise and "UNLEASH THE CHAMPION IN YOU" I know that stepping out on faith can be fragile, but it is worth the journey and all that GOD has for you! So keep sowing into your greatness, business, and legacy, keep giving, keep serving, and Queen never forgets to "Just Keep On Trucking" no matter the circumstance you will WIN, you will Overcome, you will not Settle.

Claim your winning season, no longer walk or claim lack, speak life every moment you can think of. Your winning season is determined by how you speak, how you think, and the mindset that you have to go after GOD promises for your life.

Promise yourself, Queen, that you will go after everything that GOD has for you, your mental health, physical health, finances, mindset, I mean everything he has promised you. Release the winner in you and let go of fear for your next level, no more sitting on the sideline wishing that you could win because you can you are capable. It is time to live in your fullness, no more sabotaging; we are letting go of everything holding us back. Take time to celebrate your small wins, but never stop going after your big ones.

"Always remember to forgive yourself, Believe in yourself and create your current future" Unknown

Queen "You are fearfully and wonderfully made" Psalms 139:14

If you like this journal don't forget to grab our book at:
womenceoswrite.com

Made in the USA
Middletown, DE
27 May 2022